_____________ 's PROCRASTINATIONS

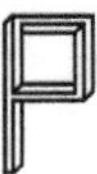

Designed & Produced by
The Studio Of NeilPowell
Copyright © 2026 All Rights Reserved.
www.neilpowell.com

This book is a structured journal intended for personal use. The content is provided for educational and informational purposes only and is not a substitute for professional advice, including medical, psychological, legal, or financial advice. The author and publisher make no representations or warranties regarding the completeness or suitability of the contents and disclaim any liability arising from its use.

ISDN: 979-8-9944172-6-3
Printed in the United States of America
This book is typeset in Manajada.

_______________________'s

PRO-
CRAS-
TINA-
TIONS

Calm Systems Vol 2
The Studio of Neil Powell

This book is not here to motivate you.

Procrastination is not laziness. It is friction. It is what happens when something feels unclear, emotionally charged, oversized, or quietly important.

Avoided tasks do not disappear. They linger. They create background noise. They take up more space than the action itself would have required.

This book is a record.

You will name what you are postponing. You will examine it. You will reduce it. Or you will release it.

Nothing more.

How to Use This Book

Start by listing your current procrastinations in the master index. Do not edit them. Write them as they appear.

Work in order.

<u>Section I</u> is for clear tasks. Small friction. Things that require movement more than analysis.

<u>Section II</u> examines why something is stuck.

<u>Section III</u> is for decisions you are postponing.

<u>Section IV</u> addresses the one thing that continues to resurface.

<u>Section V</u> allows you to formally drop what no longer belongs on your list.

You do not need to complete the book in sequence. But you should not skip the hard section.

Write plainly. Avoid drama. Avoid explanation. Be precise.

On Ranking

Not all procrastinations are equal.

Some are administrative.
Some are emotional.
Some are structural.

Ranking is not about shame. It is about clarity.

When you rank an item, you are answering:

If I handled only one thing this month, which would
change the most?

Items will move. Some will shrink. Some will dissolve.
Some will prove less important than they felt.

Re-ranking is part of the system.

Clarity reduces friction.
Friction reduces movement.
Movement reduces avoidance.

That is the cycle.

MAS
TER
LIST

Master List

#	Item	Priority	Section
		○1 ○2 ○3 ○4 ○5	I / II / III / IV / V
		○1 ○2 ○3 ○4 ○5	I / II / III / IV / V
		○1 ○2 ○3 ○4 ○5	I / II / III / IV / V
		○1 ○2 ○3 ○4 ○5	I / II / III / IV / V
		○1 ○2 ○3 ○4 ○5	I / II / III / IV / V

Section	Priority	Item	#
I / II / III / IV / V	○1 ○2 ○3 ○4 ○5		
I / II / III / IV / V	○1 ○2 ○3 ○4 ○5		
I / II / III / IV / V	○1 ○2 ○3 ○4 ○5		
I / II / III / IV / V	○1 ○2 ○3 ○4 ○5		
I / II / III / IV / V	○1 ○2 ○3 ○4 ○5		

Master List

#	Item	Priority	Section
		◯1 ◯2 ◯3 ◯4 ◯5	I / II / III / IV / V
		◯1 ◯2 ◯3 ◯4 ◯5	I / II / III / IV / V
		◯1 ◯2 ◯3 ◯4 ◯5	I / II / III / IV / V
		◯1 ◯2 ◯3 ◯4 ◯5	I / II / III / IV / V
		◯1 ◯2 ◯3 ◯4 ◯5	I / II / III / IV / V

Section	Priority	Item	#
I / II / III / IV / V	○1 ○2 ○3 ○4 ○5		
I / II / III / IV / V	○1 ○2 ○3 ○4 ○5		
I / II / III / IV / V	○1 ○2 ○3 ○4 ○5		
I / II / III / IV / V	○1 ○2 ○3 ○4 ○5		
I / II / III / IV / V	○1 ○2 ○3 ○4 ○5		

Master List

#	Item	Priority	Section
		○1 ○2 ○3 ○4 ○5	I / II / III / IV / V
		○1 ○2 ○3 ○4 ○5	I / II / III / IV / V
		○1 ○2 ○3 ○4 ○5	I / II / III / IV / V
		○1 ○2 ○3 ○4 ○5	I / II / III / IV / V
		○1 ○2 ○3 ○4 ○5	I / II / III / IV / V

Master List

Section	Priority	Item	#
I / II / III / IV / V	○1 ○2 ○3 ○4 ○5		
I / II / III / IV / V	○1 ○2 ○3 ○4 ○5		
I / II / III / IV / V	○1 ○2 ○3 ○4 ○5		
I / II / III / IV / V	○1 ○2 ○3 ○4 ○5		
I / II / III / IV / V	○1 ○2 ○3 ○4 ○5		

Master List

#	Item	Priority	Section
		○1 ○2 ○3 ○4 ○5	I / II / III / IV / V
		○1 ○2 ○3 ○4 ○5	I / II / III / IV / V
		○1 ○2 ○3 ○4 ○5	I / II / III / IV / V
		○1 ○2 ○3 ○4 ○5	I / II / III / IV / V
		○1 ○2 ○3 ○4 ○5	I / II / III / IV / V

Master List

Section	Priority	Item	#
I / II / III / IV / V	○1 ○2 ○3 ○4 ○5		
I / II / III / IV / V	○1 ○2 ○3 ○4 ○5		
I / II / III / IV / V	○1 ○2 ○3 ○4 ○5		
I / II / III / IV / V	○1 ○2 ○3 ○4 ○5		
I / II / III / IV / V	○1 ○2 ○3 ○4 ○5		

Master List

#	Item	Priority	Section
		○1 ○2 ○3 ○4 ○5	I / II / III / IV / V
		○1 ○2 ○3 ○4 ○5	I / II / III / IV / V
		○1 ○2 ○3 ○4 ○5	I / II / III / IV / V
		○1 ○2 ○3 ○4 ○5	I / II / III / IV / V
		○1 ○2 ○3 ○4 ○5	I / II / III / IV / V

Section	Priority	Item	#
I / II / III / IV / V	○1 ○2 ○3 ○4 ○5		
I / II / III / IV / V	○1 ○2 ○3 ○4 ○5		
I / II / III / IV / V	○1 ○2 ○3 ○4 ○5		
I / II / III / IV / V	○1 ○2 ○3 ○4 ○5		
I / II / III / IV / V	○1 ○2 ○3 ○4 ○5		

QUIET AVOIDANCES

Item

| Date First Avoided | |

Why I'm Delaying

Quiet Avoidances

First Small Action

Deadline (if any)

Status

○ Pending   ○ Active   ○ Done

Notes

Item

Date First Avoided

Why I'm Delaying

First Small Action

Deadline (if any)

Status

○ Pending   ○ Active   ○ Done

Notes

Date First Avoided

Why I'm Delaying

Quiet Avoidances

First Small Action

Deadline (if any)

Status

○ Pending   ○ Active   ○ Done

Notes

Item

Date First Avoided

Why I'm Delaying

Deadline (if any)

Status

◯ Pending   ◯ Active   ◯ Done

Notes

Quiet Avoidances

Item

Date First Avoided

Why I'm Delaying

Quiet Avoidances

First Small Action

Deadline (if any)

Status

○ Pending   ○ Active   ○ Done

Notes

Item

Date First Avoided

Why I'm Delaying

First Small Action

Deadline (if any)

Status

○ Pending   ○ Active   ○ Done

Notes

Item

First Small Action

Deadline (if any)

Status

○ Pending   ○ Active   ○ Done

Notes

Item

| Date First Avoided | |

| Why I'm Delaying | |

First Small Action

Deadline (if any)

○ Pending   ○ Active   ○ Done

Notes

Quiet Avoidances

Item

Date First Avoided

Why I'm Delaying

Quiet Avoidances

First Small Action

Deadline (if any)

Status

○ Pending   ○ Active   ○ Done

Notes

Item

Date First Avoided

Why I'm Delaying

Deadline (if any)

Status

○ Pending   ○ Active   ○ Done

Notes

Quiet Avoidances

Item

Date First Avoided

Why I'm Delaying

First Small Action

Deadline (if any)

Status

○ Pending   ○ Active   ○ Done

Notes

Item

Date First Avoided

Why I'm Delaying

Deadline (if any)

Status

○ Pending   ○ Active   ○ Done

Notes

Item

Date First Avoided

Why I'm Delaying

Deadline (if any)

Status

○ Pending   ○ Active   ○ Done

Notes

Quiet Avoidances

Item

Date First Avoided

Why I'm Delaying

First Small Action

Deadline (if any)

Status

○ Pending   ○ Active   ○ Done

Notes

Item

Date First Avoided

Why I'm Delaying

Deadline (if any)

Status

○ Pending   ○ Active   ○ Done

Notes

Quiet Avoidances

WHY THIS IS STUCK

Diagnosis Item:

What I believe will happen if I start:

What I believe will happen if I finish:

What happens if I do nothing?

Is This

- ○ Ambiguity
- ○ Fear of judgement
- ○ Perfectionism
- ○ Bordom

- ○ Resentment
- ○ Decision fatigue
- ○ Lack of skill
- ○ Something else

Why This Is Stuck

What would make this 10% easier?

What information am I missing?

Who could I ask?

Could This Be

○ Shortened

○ Scheduled

○ Delegated

○ Abandoned

Why This Is Stuck

Diagnosis Item:

What I believe will happen if I start:

What I believe will happen if I finish:

What happens if I do nothing?

Is This

- ○ Ambiguity
- ○ Fear of judgement
- ○ Perfectionism
- ○ Bordom

- ○ Resentment
- ○ Decision fatigue
- ○ Lack of skill
- ○ Something else

Why This Is Stuck

What would make this 10% easier?

What information am I missing?

Who could I ask?

Could This Be

○ Shortened   ○ Delegated

○ Scheduled   ○ Abandoned

Diagnosis   Item:

What I believe will happen if I start:

What I believe will happen if I finish:

What happens if I do nothing?

Is This

○ Ambiguity   ○ Resentment

○ Fear of judgement ○ Decision fatigue

○ Perfectionism   ○ Lack of skill

○ Bordom   ○ Something else

____

Why This Is Stuck

What would make this 10% easier?

What information am I missing?

Who could I ask?

Could This Be

○ Shortened   ○ Delegated

○ Scheduled   ○ Abandoned

Why This Is Stuck

Diagnosis Item:

What I believe will happen if I start:

What I believe will happen if I finish:

What happens if I do nothing?

Is This

- ○ Ambiguity
- ○ Fear of judgement
- ○ Perfectionism
- ○ Bordom
- ○ Resentment
- ○ Decision fatigue
- ○ Lack of skill
- ○ Something else

____

Why This Is Stuck

What would make this 10% easier?

What information am I missing?

Who could I ask?

Could This Be

○ Shortened   ○ Delegated

○ Scheduled   ○ Abandoned

Why This Is Stuck

Diagnosis Item:

What I believe will happen if I start:

What I believe will happen if I finish:

What happens if I do nothing?

Is This

- ○ Ambiguity
- ○ Fear of judgement
- ○ Perfectionism
- ○ Bordom

- ○ Resentment
- ○ Decision fatigue
- ○ Lack of skill
- ○ Something else

Why This Is Stuck

What would make this 10% easier?

What information am I missing?

Who could I ask?

Could This Be

○ Shortened ○ Delegated

○ Scheduled ○ Abandoned

Diagnosis

Item:

What I believe will happen if I start:

What I believe will happen if I finish:

What happens if I do nothing?

Is This

- ○ Ambiguity
- ○ Fear of judgement
- ○ Perfectionism
- ○ Bordom

- ○ Resentment
- ○ Decision fatigue
- ○ Lack of skill
- ○ Something else

____

Why This Is Stuck

What would make this 10% easier?

What information am I missing?

Who could I ask?

Could This Be

○ Shortened   ○ Delegated

○ Scheduled   ○ Abandoned

Diagnosis

Item:

What I believe will happen if I start:

What I believe will happen if I finish:

What happens if I do nothing?

Is This

- ○ Ambiguity
- ○ Fear of judgement
- ○ Perfectionism
- ○ Bordom
- ○ Resentment
- ○ Decision fatigue
- ○ Lack of skill
- ○ Something else _______________

Why This Is Stuck

What would make this 10% easier?

What information am I missing?

Who could I ask?

Could This Be

○ Shortened   ○ Delegated

○ Scheduled   ○ Abandoned

Diagnosis

Item:

What I believe will happen if I start:

What I believe will happen if I finish:

What happens if I do nothing?

Is This

- ○ Ambiguity
- ○ Fear of judgement
- ○ Perfectionism
- ○ Bordom

- ○ Resentment
- ○ Decision fatigue
- ○ Lack of skill
- ○ Something else

Why This Is Stuck

What would make this 10% easier?

What information am I missing?

Who could I ask?

Could This Be

○ Shortened   ○ Delegated

○ Scheduled   ○ Abandoned

Diagnosis

Item:

What I believe will happen if I start:

What I believe will happen if I finish:

What happens if I do nothing?

Is This

○ Ambiguity

○ Fear of judgement

○ Perfectionism

○ Bordom

○ Resentment

○ Decision fatigue

○ Lack of skill

○ Something else

____

Why This Is Stuck

What would make this 10% easier?

What information am I missing?

Who could I ask?

Could This Be

○ Shortened　　　　○ Delegated

○ Scheduled　　　　○ Abandoned

Why This Is Stuck

Diagnosis   Item:

What I believe will happen if I start:

What I believe will happen if I finish:

What happens if I do nothing?

Is This

- ○ Ambiguity
- ○ Fear of judgement
- ○ Perfectionism
- ○ Bordom

- ○ Resentment
- ○ Decision fatigue
- ○ Lack of skill
- ○ Something else _______________

Why This Is Stuck

What would make this 10% easier?

What information am I missing?

Who could I ask?

Could This Be

○ Shortened   ○ Delegated

○ Scheduled   ○ Abandoned

Diagnosis

Item:

What I believe will happen if I start:

What I believe will happen if I finish:

What happens if I do nothing?

Is This

- ○ Ambiguity
- ○ Fear of judgement
- ○ Perfectionism
- ○ Bordom

- ○ Resentment
- ○ Decision fatigue
- ○ Lack of skill
- ○ Something else

Why This Is Stuck

What would make this 10% easier?

What information am I missing?

Who could I ask?

Could This Be

○ Shortened   ○ Delegated

○ Scheduled   ○ Abandoned

Diagnosis   Item:

What I believe will happen if I start:

What I believe will happen if I finish:

What happens if I do nothing?

Is This

- ○ Ambiguity
- ○ Fear of judgement
- ○ Perfectionism
- ○ Bordom

- ○ Resentment
- ○ Decision fatigue
- ○ Lack of skill
- ○ Something else ______

Why This Is Stuck

What would make this 10% easier?

What information am I missing?

Who could I ask?

Could This Be

○ Shortened   ○ Delegated

○ Scheduled   ○ Abandoned

Diagnosis   Item:

What I believe will happen if I start:

What I believe will happen if I finish:

What happens if I do nothing?

Is This

- ○ Ambiguity
- ○ Fear of judgement
- ○ Perfectionism
- ○ Bordom

- ○ Resentment
- ○ Decision fatigue
- ○ Lack of skill
- ○ Something else ___________

Why This Is Stuck

What would make this 10% easier?

What information am I missing?

Who could I ask?

Could This Be

○ Shortened   ○ Delegated

○ Scheduled   ○ Abandoned

Diagnosis Item:

What I believe will happen if I start:

What I believe will happen if I finish:

What happens if I do nothing?

Is This

- ○ Ambiguity
- ○ Fear of judgement
- ○ Perfectionism
- ○ Bordom

- ○ Resentment
- ○ Decision fatigue
- ○ Lack of skill
- ○ Something else

____

Why This Is Stuck

What would make this 10% easier?

What information am I missing?

Who could I ask?

Could This Be

○ Shortened　　　　○ Delegated

○ Scheduled　　　　○ Abandoned

Why This Is Stuck

DESICI-SIONS I'M POST-PON-ING

The Decision

What are the real options?

What happens if I do nothing?

Worst-case scenario | Best-case scenario

Most-likely scenario

Decisions I Am Postponing

What would future-me advise?

If I had to choose in 48 hours, what would I do?

What additional data would actually change this?

Decision Date	

Status

○ Chosen   ○ Deferred   ○ No Longer Relevant

The Decision

What are the real options?

What happens if I do nothing?

Worst-case scenario

Best-case scenario

Most-likely scenario

What would future-me advise?

If I had to choose in 48 hours, what would I do?

What additional data would actually change this?

Decision Date

Status

○ Chosen   ○ Deferred   ○ No Longer Relevant

Decisions I Am Postponing

The Decision

What are the real options?

What happens if I do nothing?

Worst-case scenario

Best-case scenario

Most-likely scenario

Decisions I Am Postponing

What would future-me advise?

If I had to choose in 48 hours, what would I do?

What additional data would actually change this?

Decision Date	

Status

○ Chosen   ○ Deferred   ○ No Longer Relevant

The Decision

What are the real options?

What happens if I do nothing?

Worst-case scenario

Best-case scenario

Most-likely scenario

What would future-me advise?

If I had to choose in 48 hours, what would I do?

What additional data would actually change this?

Decision Date	

Status

○ Chosen   ○ Deferred   ○ No Longer Relevant

Decisions I Am Postponing

The Decision

What are the real options?

What happens if I do nothing?

Worst-case scenario

Best-case scenario

Most-likely scenario

What would future-me advise?

If I had to choose in 48 hours, what would I do?

What additional data would actually change this?

Decision Date	

Status

○ Chosen   ○ Deferred   ○ No Longer Relevant

The Decision

What are the real options?

What happens if I do nothing?

Worst-case scenario

Best-case scenario

Most-likely scenario

What would future-me advise?

If I had to choose in 48 hours, what would I do?

What additional data would actually change this?

Decision Date	

Status

○ Chosen   ○ Deferred   ○ No Longer Relevant

The Decision

What are the real options?

What happens if I do nothing?

Worst-case scenario

Best-case scenario

Most-likely scenario

What would future-me advise?

If I had to choose in 48 hours, what would I do?

What additional data would actually change this?

Decision Date	

Status

○ Chosen   ○ Deferred   ○ No Longer Relevant

The Decision

What are the real options?

What happens if I do nothing?

Worst-case scenario	Best-case scenario

Most-likely scenario

What would future-me advise?

If I had to choose in 48 hours, what would I do?

What additional data would actually change this?

Decision Date	

Status

○ Chosen   ○ Deferred   ○ No Longer Relevant

The Decision

What are the real options?

What happens if I do nothing?

Worst-case scenario

Best-case scenario

Most-likely scenario

What would future-me advise?

If I had to choose in 48 hours, what would I do?

What additional data would actually change this?

Decision Date	

Status

○ Chosen   ○ Deferred   ○ No Longer Relevant

The Decision

What are the real options?

What happens if I do nothing?

Worst-case scenario

Best-case scenario

Most-likely scenario

What would future-me advise?

If I had to choose in 48 hours, what would I do?

What additional data would actually change this?

Decision Date

Status

○ Chosen   ○ Deferred   ○ No Longer Relevant

The Decision

What are the real options?

What happens if I do nothing?

Worst-case scenario

Best-case scenario

Most-likely scenario

What would future-me advise?

If I had to choose in 48 hours, what would I do?

What additional data would actually change this?

Decision Date	

Status

○ Chosen   ○ Deferred   ○ No Longer Relevant

The Decision

What are the real options?

What happens if I do nothing?

Worst-case scenario

Best-case scenario

Most-likely scenario

What would future-me advise?

If I had to choose in 48 hours, what would I do?

What additional data would actually change this?

Decision Date	

Status

○ Chosen   ○ Deferred   ○ No Longer Relevant

The Decision

What are the real options?

What happens if I do nothing?

Worst-case scenario	Best-case scenario

Most-likely scenario

What would future-me advise?

If I had to choose in 48 hours, what would I do?

What additional data would actually change this?

Decision Date	

Status

○ Chosen   ○ Deferred   ○ No Longer Relevant

The Decision

What are the real options?

What happens if I do nothing?

Worst-case scenario

Best-case scenario

Most-likely scenario

What would future-me advise?

If I had to choose in 48 hours, what would I do?

What additional data would actually change this?

Decision Date

Status

○ Chosen   ○ Deferred   ○ No Longer Relevant

Decisions I Am Postponing

The Decision

What are the real options?

What happens if I do nothing?

Worst-case scenario | Best-case scenario

Most-likely scenario

What would future-me advise?

If I had to choose in 48 hours, what would I do?

What additional data would actually change this?

Decision Date

Status

○ Chosen   ○ Deferred   ○ No Longer Relevant

The Decision

What are the real options?

What happens if I do nothing?

Worst-case scenario	Best-case scenario

Most-likely scenario

What would future-me advise?

If I had to choose in 48 hours, what would I do?

What additional data would actually change this?

Decision Date	

Status

○ Chosen   ○ Deferred   ○ No Longer Relevant

THE ONE I'M AVOIDING RIGHT NOW

The Thing

How long have I been avoiding this?

○ Weeks   ○ Months   ○ Year

Why this matters

What continues to happen because I delay this?

○ Money Leakage   ○ Identity drift   ○ Stress background noise
○ Strain in relationship   ○ Loss of opportunity   ○ Something else: __________

Estimated cost of another 3 months of avoidance

Worst realistic out come if I start

Most likely scenario if I start

Reduce It to Motion

Break the imtimidation cycle.

What would count as "started"?
(Define the threshold) **1**

The first 15 minutes of action **2**

What is the smallest irreverssible step? **3**
(Email sent. Appointment booked. Money transferred. File created.)

When will I begin?	Date	Time

Done?

○ Yes   ○ Not yet

Anxiety level before starting (1-10) _____

Anxiety level after starting (1-10) _____

The One I'm Avoiding Right Now

The Thing

How long have I been avoiding this?

○ Weeks   ○ Months   ○ Year

Why this matters

What continues to happen because I delay this?

○ Money Leakage   ○ Identity drift   ○ Stress background noise
○ Strain in relationship   ○ Loss of opportunity   ○ Something else: _________

Estimated cost of another 3 months of avoidance

Worst realistic out come if I start

Most likely scenario if I start

The One I'm Avoiding Right Now

Reduce It to Motion

What would count as "started"?
(Define the threshold)

1

The first 15 minutes of action

2

What is the smallest irreverssible step?
(Email sent. Appointment booked. Money transferred. File created.)

3

When will I begin?	Date	Time

Done?

○ Yes   ○ Not yet

Anxiety level before starting (1-10) ＿＿

Anxiety level after starting (1-10) ＿＿

The One I'm Avoiding Right Now

The Thing

How long have I been avoiding this?

○ Weeks   ○ Months   ○ Year

Why this matters

What continues to happen because I delay this?

○ Money Leakage   ○ Identity drift   ○ Stress background noise
○ Strain in relationship ○ Loss of opportunity   ○ Something else: __________

Estimated cost of another 3 months of avoidance

Worst realistic out come if I start

Most likely scenario if I start

The One I'm Avoiding Right Now

Reduce It to Motion

Break the imtimidation cycle.

What would count as "started"?
(Define the threshold)

1

The first 15 minutes of action

2

What is the smallest irreverssible step?
(Email sent. Appointment booked. Money transferred. File created.)

3

When will I begin?	Date	Time

Done?

○ Yes   ○ Not yet

Anxiety level before starting (1-10) _____

Anxiety level after starting (1-10) _____

The One I'm Avoiding Right Now

The Thing

How long have I been avoiding this?

○ Weeks   ○ Months   ○ Year

Why this matters

What continues to happen because I delay this?

○ Money Leakage   ○ Identity drift   ○ Stress background noise
○ Strain in relationship   ○ Loss of opportunity   ○ Something else: __________

Estimated cost of another 3 months of avoidance

Worst realistic out come if I start

Most likely scenario if I start

Break the imtimidation cycle.

1 What would count as "started"?
(Define the threshold)

2 The first 15 minutes of action

3 What is the smallest irreverssible step?
(Email sent. Appointment booked. Money transferred. File created.)

When will I begin?	Date	Time

Done?

○ Yes   ○ Not yet

Anxiety level before starting (1-10) ____

Anxiety level after starting (1-10) ____

The One I'm Avoiding Right Now

The Thing

How long have I been avoiding this?

○ Weeks   ○ Months   ○ Year

Why this matters

What continues to happen because I delay this?

○ Money Leakage   ○ Identity drift   ○ Stress background noise
○ Strain in relationship   ○ Loss of opportunity   ○ Something else: __________

Estimated cost of another 3 months of avoidance

Worst realistic out come if I start

Most likely scenario if I start

The One I'm Avoiding Right Now

Reduce It to Motion

Break the imtimidation cycle.

What would count as "started"?
(Define the threshold) | 1

The first 15 minutes of action | 2

What is the smallest irreverssible step?
(Email sent. Appointment booked. Money transferred. File created.) | 3

When will I begin?	Date	Time

Done?

○ Yes   ○ Not yet

Anxiety level before starting (1-10) _____

Anxiety level after starting (1-10) _____

The One I'm Avoiding Right Now

The Thing

How long have I been avoiding this?

○ Weeks   ○ Months   ○ Year

Why this matters

What continues to happen because I delay this?

○ Money Leakage   ○ Identity drift   ○ Stress background noise
○ Strain in relationship   ○ Loss of opportunity   ○ Something else: __________

Estimated cost of another 3 months of avoidance

Worst realistic out come if I start

Most likely scenario if I start

Reduce It to Motion

Break the imtimidation cycle.

What would count as "started"?
(Define the threshold)

1

The first 15 minutes of action

2

What is the smallest irreverssible step?
(Email sent. Appointment booked. Money transferred. File created.)

3

When will I begin?	Date	Time

Done?

○ Yes   ○ Not yet

Anxiety level before starting (1-10) _____

Anxiety level after starting (1-10) _____

The One I'm Avoiding Right Now

The Thing

How long have I been avoiding this?

◯ Weeks   ◯ Months   ◯ Year

Why this matters

What continues to happen because I delay this?

◯ Money Leakage   ◯ Identity drift   ◯ Stress background noise
◯ Strain in relationship   ◯ Loss of opportunity   ◯ Something else: __________

Estimated cost of another 3 months of avoidance

Worst realistic out come if I start

Most likely scenario if I start

The One I'm Avoiding Right Now

Reduce It to Motion

Break the imtimidation cycle.

What would count as "started"? | **1**
(Define the threshold)

The first 15 minutes of action | **2**

What is the smallest irreverssible step? | **3**
(Email sent. Appointment booked. Money transferred. File created.)

When will I begin?	Date	Time

Done?

○ Yes   ○ Not yet

Anxiety level before starting (1-10) ____

Anxiety level after starting (1-10) ____

The One I'm Avoiding Right Now

The Thing

How long have I been avoiding this?

○ Weeks   ○ Months   ○ Year

Why this matters

What continues to happen because I delay this?

○ Money Leakage   ○ Identity drift   ○ Stress background noise
○ Strain in relationship   ○ Loss of opportunity   ○ Something else: __________

Estimated cost of another 3 months of avoidance

Worst realistic out come if I start

Most likely scenario if I start

The One I'm Avoiding Right Now

Reduce It to Motion

Break the imtimidation cycle.

What would count as "started"?
(Define the threshold)

1

The first 15 minutes of action

2

What is the smallest irreverssible step?
(Email sent. Appointment booked. Money transferred. File created.)

3

When will I begin?	Date	Time

Done?

○ Yes   ○ Not yet

Anxiety level before starting (1-10) _____

Anxiety level after starting (1-10) _____

The One I'm Avoiding Right Now

The Thing

How long have I been avoiding this?

○ Weeks   ○ Months   ○ Year

Why this matters

What continues to happen because I delay this?

○ Money Leakage   ○ Identity drift   ○ Stress background noise
○ Strain in relationship   ○ Loss of opportunity   ○ Something else: __________

Estimated cost of another 3 months of avoidance

Worst realistic out come if I start

Most likely scenario if I start

Reduce It to Motion

What would count as "started"?
(Define the threshold)

1

The first 15 minutes of action

2

What is the smallest irreverssible step?
(Email sent. Appointment booked. Money transferred. File created.)

3

When will I begin?	Date	Time

Done?

○ Yes   ○ Not yet

Anxiety level before starting (1-10) ____

Anxiety level after starting (1-10) ____

The One I'm Avoiding Right Now

The Thing

How long have I been avoiding this?

◯ Weeks   ◯ Months   ◯ Year

Why this matters

What continues to happen because I delay this?

◯ Money Leakage   ◯ Identity drift   ◯ Stress background noise
◯ Strain in relationship   ◯ Loss of opportunity   ◯ Something else: __________

Estimated cost of another 3 months of avoidance

Worst realistic out come if I start

Most likely scenario if I start

The One I'm Avoiding Right Now

Reduce It to Motion

Break the imtimidation cycle.

What would count as "started"? | **1**
(Define the threshold)

The first 15 minutes of action | **2**

What is the smallest irreverssible step? | **3**
(Email sent. Appointment booked. Money transferred. File created.)

When will I begin?	Date	Time

Done?

○ Yes   ○ Not yet

Anxiety level before starting (1-10) _____

Anxiety level after starting (1-10) _____

The One I'm Avoiding Right Now

The Thing

How long have I been avoiding this?

○ Weeks   ○ Months   ○ Year

Why this matters

What continues to happen because I delay this?

○ Money Leakage   ○ Identity drift   ○ Stress background noise

○ Strain in relationship   ○ Loss of opportunity   ○ Something else: __________

Estimated cost of another 3 months of avoidance

Worst realistic out come if I start

Most likely scenario if I start

The One I'm Avoiding Right Now

Reduce It to Motion

Break the imtimidation cycle.

What would count as "started"?
(Define the threshold)

1

The first 15 minutes of action

2

What is the smallest irreverssible step?
(Email sent. Appointment booked. Money transferred. File created.)

3

When will I begin?	Date	Time

Done?

○ Yes   ○ Not yet

Anxiety level before starting (1-10) _____

Anxiety level after starting (1-10) _____

The One I'm Avoiding Right Now

The Thing

How long have I been avoiding this?

○ Weeks   ○ Months   ○ Year

Why this matters

What continues to happen because I delay this?

○ Money Leakage   ○ Identity drift   ○ Stress background noise
○ Strain in relationship   ○ Loss of opportunity   ○ Something else: __________

Estimated cost of another 3 months of avoidance

Worst realistic out come if I start

Most likely scenario if I start

Reduce It to Motion

What would count as "started"? | **1**
(Define the threshold)

The first 15 minutes of action | **2**

What is the smallest irreverssible step? | **3**
(Email sent. Appointment booked. Money transferred. File created.)

When will I begin?	Date	Time

Done?

○ Yes   ○ Not yet

Anxiety level before starting (1-10) ____

Anxiety level after starting (1-10) ____

The One I'm Avoiding Right Now

The Thing

How long have I been avoiding this?

○ Weeks   ○ Months   ○ Year

Why this matters

What continues to happen because I delay this?

○ Money Leakage   ○ Identity drift   ○ Stress background noise
○ Strain in relationship   ○ Loss of opportunity   ○ Something else: __________

Estimated cost of another 3 months of avoidance

Worst realistic out come if I start

Most likely scenario if I start

Reduce It to Motion

Break the imtimidation cycle.

What would count as "started"? | **1**
(Define the threshold)

The first 15 minutes of action | **2**

What is the smallest irreverssible step? | **3**
(Email sent. Appointment booked. Money transferred. File created.)

When will I begin?	Date	Time

Done?

○ Yes   ○ Not yet

Anxiety level before starting (1-10) ____

Anxiety level after starting (1-10) ____

The One I'm Avoiding Right Now

The Thing

How long have I been avoiding this?

○ Weeks   ○ Months   ○ Year

Why this matters

What continues to happen because I delay this?

○ Money Leakage   ○ Identity drift   ○ Stress background noise
○ Strain in relationship   ○ Loss of opportunity   ○ Something else: ___________

Estimated cost of another 3 months of avoidance

Worst realistic out come if I start

Most likely scenario if I start

The One I'm Avoiding Right Now

Reduce It to Motion

Break the imtimidation cycle.

What would count as "started"?
(Define the threshold)

1

The first 15 minutes of action

2

What is the smallest irreverssible step?
(Email sent. Appointment booked. Money transferred. File created.)

3

When will I begin?	Date	Time

Done?

○ Yes   ○ Not yet

Anxiety level before starting (1-10) _____

Anxiety level after starting (1-10) _____

The One I'm Avoiding Right Now

AR-CHIVE

Item

Date First Listed	
Date Resolved	

How long have I been avoiding this?

○ Weeks   ○ Months   ○ Year

What changed once this was handled?

Was it as difficult as expected?

○ More   ○ About the same   ○ Less

Would I avoid this again?

Archive

Item

Date First Listed	
Date Resolved	

How long have I been avoiding this?

○ Weeks   ○ Months   ○ Year

What changed once this was handled?

Was it as difficult as expected?

○ More   ○ About the same   ○ Less

Would I avoid this again?

Archive

Item

Date First Listed	
Date Resolved	

How long have I been avoiding this?

○ Weeks   ○ Months   ○ Year

What changed once this was handled?

Was it as difficult as expected?

○ More   ○ About the same   ○ Less

Would I avoid this again?

Item

Date First Listed	
Date Resolved	

How long have I been avoiding this?

○ Weeks   ○ Months   ○ Year

What changed once this was handled?

Was it as difficult as expected?

○ More   ○ About the same   ○ Less

Would I avoid this again?

Archive

Item

Date First Listed	
Date Resolved	

How long have I been avoiding this?

○ Weeks   ○ Months   ○ Year

What changed once this was handled?

Was it as difficult as expected?

○ More   ○ About the same   ○ Less

Would I avoid this again?

Item

Date First Listed	
Date Resolved	

How long have I been avoiding this?

○ Weeks   ○ Months   ○ Year

What changed once this was handled?

Was it as difficult as expected?

○ More   ○ About the same   ○ Less

Would I avoid this again?

Archive

Item

Date First Listed	
Date Resolved	

How long have I been avoiding this?

○ Weeks   ○ Months   ○ Year

What changed once this was handled?

Was it as difficult as expected?

○ More   ○ About the same   ○ Less

Would I avoid this again?

Archive

Item

Date First Listed	

Date Resolved	

How long have I been avoiding this?

○ Weeks　　　　○ Months　　　　○ Year

What changed once this was handled?

Was it as difficult as expected?

○ More　　　　○ About the same　　　　○ Less

Would I avoid this again?

Archive

Item

Date First Listed	
Date Resolved	

How long have I been avoiding this?

○ Weeks   ○ Months   ○ Year

What changed once this was handled?

Was it as difficult as expected?

○ More   ○ About the same   ○ Less

Would I avoid this again?

Item

Date First Listed	
Date Resolved	

How long have I been avoiding this?

○ Weeks   ○ Months   ○ Year

What changed once this was handled?

Was it as difficult as expected?

○ More   ○ About the same   ○ Less

Would I avoid this again?

Archive

Avoidance shrinks when named.